Split Field Coverages

Jerry Gordon

DEDICATION

This book is dedicated to all the players I have coached. It wouldn't have been possible without you. Doesn't Matter, Get Better. This book is also dedicated to my wife, Carol. Thank you for your enduring support. Love you more than you know.

CONTENTS

Acknowledgments

ACKNOWLEDGMENTS

Thank you to all the coaches that helped me through the years. I would especially like to thank John Strollo and Jerry Azzinaro. I try to live up to the standards you set for me many years ago. Thank you to Keith Kenyon, Chris Gilderhaus, and Mitch Griffis for your editing ideas

1 SPLIT FIELD INTRODUCTION

I decided to write this book as a sequel to "Coaching the Under Front Defense", a book I wrote several years ago. I wrote "Coaching the Under Front Defense" because I could not find a comprehensive source of information about the topic. Football, as we all know, evolves in cycles and is evolving much faster now due to the resources one can easily find on the Internet. Although you can find numerous articles about spilt field coverages, many, if not most, assume you know their terminology, don't explain their terminology in a concise manner, or assume you know more information than you actually know. This book is meant to provide a primer on the subject. Very simply, Split Field Coverage means that there will be 2 coverage calls, independent of each other, made by the safeties on every play. The coverage calls are based on the formation the offense presents, allowing the defense to hold the chalk last before the ball is snapped.

It is my hope that you will use this book as a guide, taking from a menu of items, ideas that you will be actually able to use at the HIGH SCHOOL level. Everything in this book, I have learned from others and have actually used in a game or practice situation, or intend to do so in the future. Please note, there are many ways to play split field coverage. This just happens to be, for me, the easiest way to teach it to high school players and to be able to simply FIX it during the heat of battle. The great advantage of using a split field system is that it allows you to tailor the defense to YOUR specific situation.

Why Split Field Coverage

Split field coverages allow you to have simple premade answers for many of the formation problems an offense can present. Once taught, split field coverage gives you tools and options that can be adjusted from week to week. Most importantly, with the advent of sideline technology, you will be able to adjust from series to series during games. I hope that you take these tools and utilize in your program to solve the multitude of problems offenses present each week.

2 BASIC TERMINOLOGY

S- The Sam is an outside linebacker that aligns to the field
E- The End is the defensive end that is aligned on the same
side as the Sam.
N- The Nose is aligned on the same side as the Sam
T- The Tackle is a defensive tackle that is aligned away from
the Sam
B- The Buck is the defensive end or an outside linebacker
 that is aligned away from the Sam.
M- The Mac is a linebacker that aligns to the side of the Sam
W- The Will is a linebacker that lines up away from the Sam
R- The Rover is a safety that lines up always lines away
from the Sam
F- The Free alignment is not tied into the front, which is why
he is called the Free
C- Corners. Corners line up left and right. Many coaches
have a field and boundary corner or have one corner follow a
particular receiver out of the huddle based on game plan.

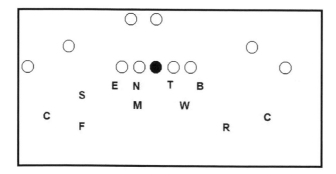

Figure 2-1. Basic Terminology.

Technique Definitions

Techniques are used to describe how a player lines up on an offensive lineman. When a 0 is added to the technique, this means that the player is on the linebacker level or second level of play. For instance, a 3 technique would mean that the player would line up outside shade of the guard. A 30 technique would be on the outside shade of the guard but at linebacker level.

Shade technique	Shade of the center
0 technique	Head up of the center
2 technique	Head up on the guard
2I technique	Inside shade of the guard
3 technique	Outside shade of the guard
4 technique	Head up on the tackle
4I technique	Inside shade of the tackle
5 technique	Outside shade of the tackle
6 technique	Head up on the tight end
7 technique	Inside shade of the tight end
9 technique	Outside shade of the tight end

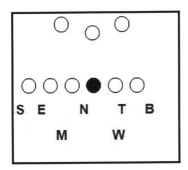

Figure 2-2. Techniques Defined.

Gap Designation

A Gap   Between the center and the guard
B Gap   Between the guard and the tackle
C Gap   Between the tackle and tight end, outside the tackle versus no tight end
D Gap   Outside the tight end

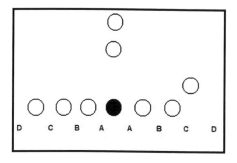

Figure 2-3. Gap designation.

Receiver Designation

#1   First receiver of the formation counting outside in
#2   The second receiver of the formation counting outside in
#3   The third receiver of the formation counting outside in

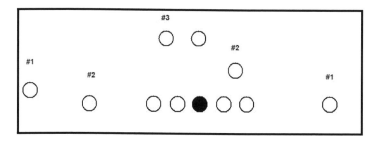

Figure 2-4. Receiver designation

5

3 SPLIT FIELD COVERAGE BASICS

Split Field coverages can be played from either a 4 down lineman defense (Figure 3-1) or a 3 down lineman defense (Figure 3-2). Many teams will play split field coverage from both looks and it is relatively simple to execute.

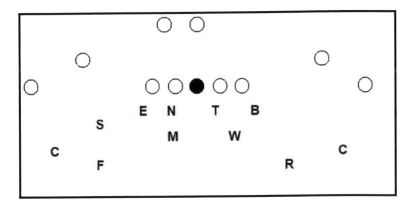

Figure 3-1. Field Defense using 4 Down Linemen

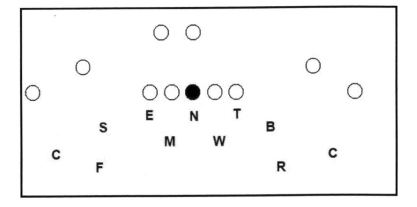

Figure 3-2. Okie Defense using 3 Down Lineman.

The structure of our call is Front, Stunt/Blitz, Coverage. An example of a call would be Field Taxi Read Choice Special. Field is the front, Taxi is the stunt, and Read Choice Special is the coverage. One defensive coach signals in the front and stunt and another coach signals in the coverage. All linebackers and defensive backs look to the sideline to receive the call. A linebacker will give the call to the defensive line.

The coverage call is broken into 3 parts: The frontside, the away side, and our check to trips. So in the call above, the frontside is playing read, the away side has a choice based on game plan, and the trips call is special. As your secondary becomes more experienced, you can drop "choice" from the call as it is always assumed the away side will have a choice of calls.

Note: many of our terms are similar to older TCU terminology but have been modified to fit the needs of high school.

Split Field Coverage Tools

Frontside Call Possibilities: Read, Robber, Trap All frontside call are made by the Free.

Away Call Possibilities: Sky, Blue, Rat All away calls are made by the Rover

Each safety will make a call based to the formation he sees to his side. The Free makes the frontside call and the Rover makes the backside call.

Again, the call is "Read, Choice, Special. This means the Free is only allowed to play Read to his side, the Rover is given a choice of Blue, Sky or Rat and we will play Special to trips. Note: you can give the Rover different choices based on your personnel or the team you are playing.

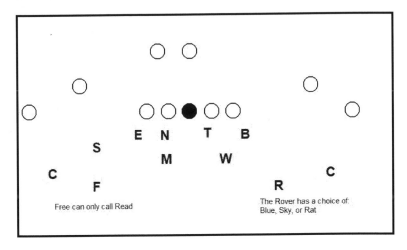

Figure 3-3. Frontside and away side calls

Let's get started!

Frontside Coverages

Frontside calls are calls that are sent in and are generally played as called, meaning if we call read, we want read to be played. Note: We have changed the way we played read over the course of years and it is different than in my previous book, "Coaching the Under Front Defense".

Read Coverage

Corner- Align: 6-8 yds deep and 1 yard inside #1. Eyes on #1

- #1 man except for shallow (2-3 yard) inside release. Make an *in* call if your receiver shallow releases.
- Drive on 3 step routes.
- Bait the 5 step hitch. Call hitch to get help from your linebacker.
- Play #1 inside and over the top
- Play #2 man when you get an out call

Free- Alignment: 8-10 yds deep and 1 yard inside #2. Eyes on #2

- #2 vertical release- Man to man . Play from an inside position
- #2 outside release- Yell out and play over the top of #1. Think fade, post, dig
- #2 inside release- Melt to 1/3 making sure #2 doesn't drive vertical, then think post. If the team you are playing doesn't run posts, have him rob #1.

Notes:
- All positions are played from an "ability" alignment.
- Vertical is defined as the receiver taking 3-4 steps off the ball.
- An out call is made when a receiver makes a cut to the outside AND the safety could cover the fade if #1 ran vertically. So, if its 3rd and 10 and the safety is aligned deeper, there would be more chance of an out call. Consequently, if the safety is aligned tighter to his man, there would be less chance of an out call because the safety would not be able to cover the fade. We use an out call system to eliminate confusion between the safety and the corner. There never should be a "he said she said". The safety is in charge. In other words, the corner should NEVER

jump the out unless he gets an out call. It is better to have to out competed than a wide open fade.

Sam - Align 5 yards deep and apex (split the difference) between the end man on the line of scrimmage (EMOL) and the next receiver. Eyes on EMOL.

- Curl to the swing of #3

The curl is defined as 10 yards deep and 1 yard inside the next outside receiver. We do this so we are dropping to a receiver and not covering grass. A common mistake a Sam will make is to leave the curl too early and jump #3 as he is coming out of the backfield, thus creating an open window to #2. Coaching Point: Hold the curl until the QB turns his shoulder to #3.

Mac: Alignment: 5 yds deep and in a 30 alignment over the guard.

Control #3.
Controlling #3 means
- Wall, collision and carry any #3 vertical.
- If #3 outside releases, watch for any inside complimentary routes to the side of the #3 release. #2 and #3 exchange.
- If #3 blocks, get depth and play under digs. This can be game plan adjusted.

  - Mac can blitz. (many coaches call this a green dog)
  - Drop to an area of the field based on the tendency of the offense.
  - Spy a quarterback that likes to run.
  - Play screens and draws.

Read Coverage vs. Common Routes

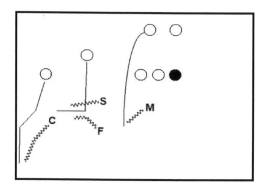

Figure 3-4. Fade, Out, Vert. Corner has fade. We play this low and inside forcing the QB to throw it over our head. This eliminates what HS QB's with weak arms call a back shoulder fade. The Free takes the deep out as he threatened our vertical. The Sam is under the out. The Mac has #3 vertical

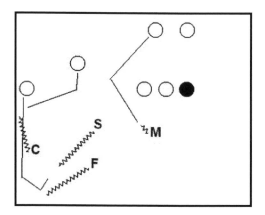

Figure 3-5. Curl, Arrow, Angle. The Free makes an "OUT" call telling the Corner to jump the arrow. The Free plays over the curl. The Sam plays under the curl. The Mac should not allow the RB to cross the formation.

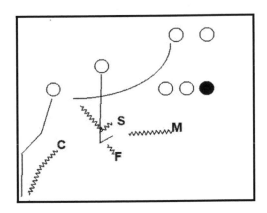

Figure 3-6. Fade, Curl, Arrow. The Corner has the fade. The Free is on top of the curl. The Sam holds the curl as long as possible looking at the QB's shoulders and eyes as to when to break on the swing of #3. The Mac expands to his new #3.

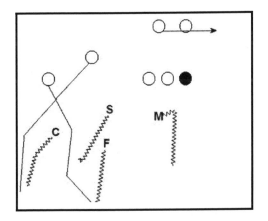

Figure 3-7. Post, Wheel, Run Fake. Corner and Free switch. The Sam drops 10-12 yards and reads QB. The Mac must honor the run fake and then drive for depth. Often times, we will tell the linebackers that get sucked up in a run fake to continue on to the QB as they are not in position to cover the pass. We say, "do not get stuck between a poop and a fart".

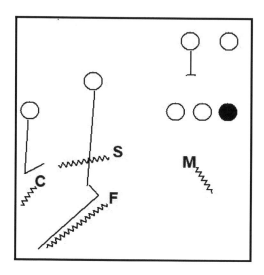

Figure 3-8. Hitch, Corner (Smash), Block. The Corner should make a "HITCH" call and position himself between the hitch and the corner route, "baiting" the QB to throw the hitch. The Free plays over the Corner. The Sam, getting the hitch call immediately, expands to the hitch. The Mac should get depth when the RB blocks. This can also be game plan adjusted.

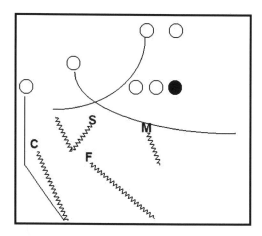

Figure 3-9. Post, Under, Arrow. The Corner plays the post. The Free calls "UNDER" and plays the middle of the field. The Sam drops to his curl and the plays the swing of #3. The Mac should try to wall the new #3 if he is more than 4 yards deep.

Robber

Corner- Align: 6-8 yds deep and 1 yard inside #1. Eyes on #1 (same alignment as Read)
- #1 man except for shallow (2-3 yard) inside release. Make an *in* call if your receiver shallow releases. You can squeeze the post
- Be late to the 5 step hitch. Call hitch to get help from your linebacker.
- Play #1 inside and over the top- Play under #2 running a corner

Free- Align 8 yards deep. Apex between the tackle and the next receiver.
- #2 vertical release- Man to man from an inside position
- #2 outside release- Rob the post, dig or curl. The curl is defined as being 2 yards inside of #1.
- #2 inside release- Melt to 1/3 making sure the tight end doesn't drive vertical, then think post. If the team you are playing doesn't run posts, have him rob #1.

Note: The big coverage difference between Read and Robber is what happens when #2 goes out. The out call is handled by an outside linebacker and the Free is now able to help the corner when #2 runs an out.

Sam- Align 5 yards deep and 1 yard outside # 2
- Maintain outside leverage on #2
- If #2 expands (runs towards the sideline), play flat/wheel. The Sam is the flat player
- If #2 doesn't expand, play the curl, listen for hitch or in call from corner, watch for #2 and #3 exchange. Many coaches have the Sam look directly to the flat now and is one change ups we will make when a team runs a lot of hitches.

Mac
Control #3.

Robber Coverage vs Common Routes

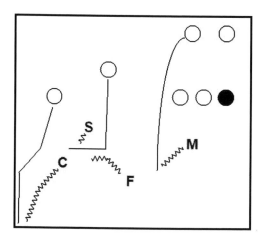

Figure 3-10. Fade, Out, Vert. Corner has fade. Free will be over the deep out. Sam will be under the deep out. The Mac has #3 vertical.

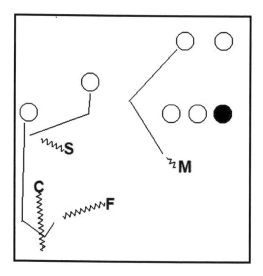

Figure 3-11. Curl, Arrow, Angle. The Corner plays on top of the curl. The Free sees #2 go out and helps with #1 playing under the curl. The Sam has the arrow. The Mac should not allow the RB to cross the formation.

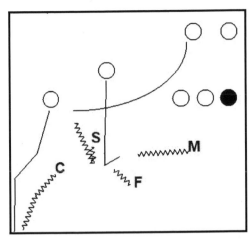

Figure 3-12. Fade, Curl, Arrow. The Corner has the fade. The Free is on top of the curl. The Sam holds the curl as long as possible looking at the QB's shoulders and eyes as to when to break on the swing of #3. The Mac expands to his new #3.

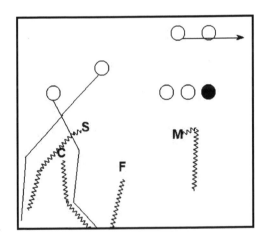

Figure 3-13. Post, Wheel, Run Fake. The Corner is over the post. The Free sees #2 go out and plays under the post. The Sam has the wheel as #2 runs through his flat The Mac must honor the run fake and then drive for depth.

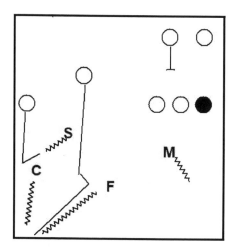

Figure 3-14. Hitch, Corner (Smash), Block. The Corner should make a "HITCH" call and play under the corner. The Free plays over the corner. The Sam, getting the hitch call, immediately expands to the hitch. The Mac should get depth when the RB blocks. This can also be game plan adjusted.

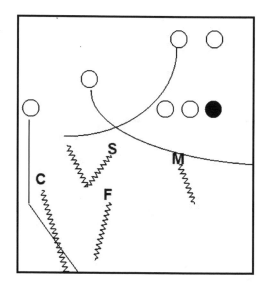

Figure 3-15. Post, Under, Arrow. The Corner plays the over the post. The Free calls "UNDER" and plays under the post. The Sam drops to his curl and the plays the swing of #3. The Mac should try to wall the new #3 if he is more than 4 yards deep.

Trap

Corner- Align 3-5 yards deep and 1 yard outside #1
- Force inside release of #1. If #1 releases outside expect 3 step fade.
- Squeeze the #1 receiver until your flat is threatened.
- If your flat is threatened soft sink and read the qb's shoulders. Play any second receiver through the flat man to man.

Free- Align 10 deep and 2 yards inside #2.
- Soft pedal with width and depth on the snap of ball.
- If #2 goes to the flat expand your drop with width.
- Deep half player.

Sam- Align 5 yards deep and apex (split the difference) between the end man on the line of scrimmage (EMOL) and the next receiver. (Same alignment as Read)
- Play Curl.
- Reroute #2 into the "hour glass". The hour glass is formed by the corner playing outside leverage and the Sam playing inside leverage on their men
- Listen for an in call from the corner

Mac
Control #3.

Trap Coverage vs Common Routes

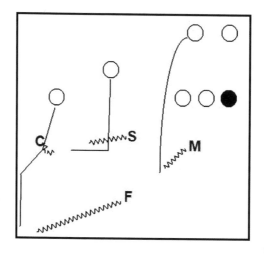

Figure 3-16. Fade, Out, Vert. Corner squeezes #1 as long as possible and plays the deep out. Free has the fade. Sam will be inside the deep out. The Mac has #3 vertical.

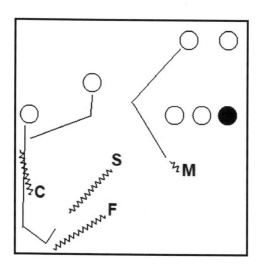

Figure 3-17. Curl, Arrow, Angle. The Corner squeezes #1 and plays the arrow. The Free is on top of the curl. The Sam is under the curl. The Mac should not allow the RB to cross the formation.

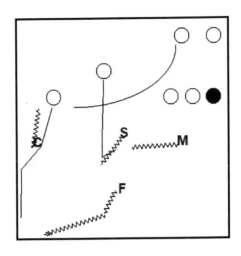

Figure 3-18. Fade, Curl, Arrow. The Corner squeezes #1 and plays the arrow. The Free plays the fade. The Sam plays the curl over the top . The Mac expands to his new #3.

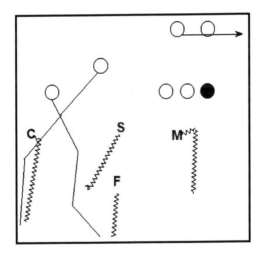

Figure 3-19. Post, Wheel, Run Fake. The Corner squeezes #1 and takes #2 man through his flat. The basic rule for a flat player is to play the second man through your flat man to man. The Free sees #2 go out and plays over the post. The Sam gets as deep as possible into his curl area looking for digs. The Mac must honor the run fake and then drive for depth.

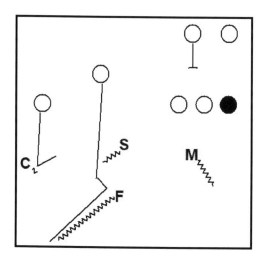

Basics 20. Hitch, Corner (Smash), Block. The Corner should make a "HITCH" call and play the hitch. The Free plays over the corner route. The Sam, getting the hitch call, can help if the hitch breaks inside. The Mac should get depth when the RB blocks. This can also be game plan adjusted.

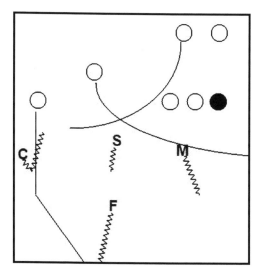

Basics 21. Post, Under, Arrow. The Corner squeezes #1 and plays the arrow. The Free calls "UNDER" and plays over the post. The Sam seeing and hearing the under call gets depth and looks for a crosser. The Mac should try to wall the new #3 if he is more than 4 yards deep.

Away side calls:

The Rover is given a choice of 3 calls to make: Blue, Sky or Rat. The Rover's base call is Sky. He makes this call anytime there are two backs in the backfield or if there is a single receiver to his side. Note: Certain trips calls will negate the sky check. See the Split Field Trips chapter for further explanation. He will call Blue if there is one back and 2 eligible receivers to his side. He will call Rat if there are three eligible receivers to his side.

Sky

Sky- Made to a single receiver and all 2 back formations. The Rover is force when making a sky call.

Rover/Sam- Alignment 2x2 off a TE and 4x5 off an OT
Low Player
- Flat to wheel

Corner- Align as you would in Read
High Player
- Play deep ½

Away Linebacker- Alignment: 5 yds deep and in a 20 alignment over the guard
Control #2 (running back to your side)

Controlling #2 means
- Wall, collision and carry any #2 vertical
- If #2 outside releases, watch for any inside complimentary routes to the side of the #2 release.
- If #2 blocks, get depth and play under digs. This can be game plan adjusted.
  - Will can blitz.
  - Drop to an area of the field based on the tendency of the offense.
  - Spy a quarterback that likes to run.
  - Play screens and draws.

Common Routes vs Sky Coverage

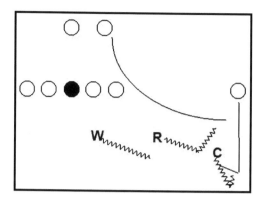

Figure 3-22. Curl, Arrow. The Corner is on top of the curl. The Rover has the flat. The Will expands to get under the curl as #2 outside releases.

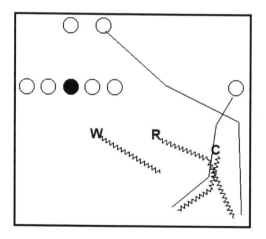

Figure 3-23. Post Wheel. The Corner plays the post. The Rover has the second man through his flat man to man (the WR would be the first man through the flat.). The Will expands and gets depth as #2 runs a wheel.

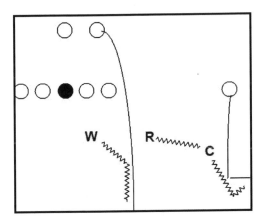

Figure 3-24. Out, Vertical. The Corner is on top of the out. The Rover would be under the out. The Will must carry #2 vertical. If the will cannot match up with #2, see Figure 3-26.

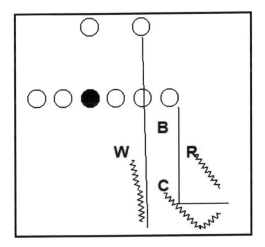

Figure 3-25. TE Out, Vertical. We play it the same way if we are facing a nub TE. The Corner is on top of the out. The Rover would be under the out. The Will must carry #2 vertical.

Blue

Blue is called by the Rover to all one back 2 receiver formations. Note if a dangerous pass catcher were to align in the backfield, we would check blue to that as well (Figure 3-26). We need to make a Blue call to tell the away backer that he is now the force player.

Blue is played exactly like read with just one exception. The exception being if #2 inside releases, the Rover plays high to low. This is done because if the offense ran both #2's underneath (mesh route) it is possible the Rover and the Free would end up in the same spot. (Figure 3-27)

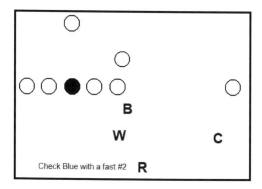

Figure 3-26. Check Blue to a fast #2 in the backfield.

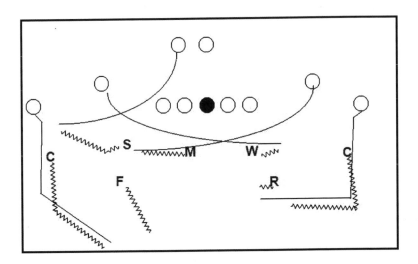

Figure 3-27. Mesh. The Corner and the Free play the post. The Free should make an "under" call. The Sam has his swing of #3. If #3 did not swing he would get depth and play under digs. The Rover calls "under" and plays digs to his side. The Mac plays the under from the Rover's side and the Will plays the under from the Sam's side.

Rat

Rat is called by the Rover when three receivers are aligned to the Rover. Rat is a form of Cover 3. We call it Rat because there are three letters in Rat, we are playing a form of Cover 3 to his side.

Corner to trips- Align between the bottom of the #'s and the sideline no closer than 5 yards from the boundary.

- Play deep 1/3
- Be a deep as the deepest and in the middle of both #1 and #2 if both release vertical. Be alert for #2 and #3 deep crossing
- Do not chase post
- Call in or hitch to the apex player if necessary. You have the remaining player deep man to man.

Rover- Alignment: Apex #2 and #3 5 yards deep
- Wall, collision and carry #2 vertical
- Come off any vertical when *in or hitch* is called by the corner.
- If #2 outside releases, play curl to flat. Playing curl to flat means that the apex player plays the curl until the quarterback's shoulders and eyes turn to the flat route. Do not run with the wheel player.

Free: Alignment 12 yards deep between the #1's on either side of the field. Deep as the deepest.

Will- Alignment: 50 over the OT
- Control #3
- Come off any vertical and play any *in* calls made by the corner or a safety
- If #3 outside releases play hook to curl

Sam: Alignment: 4x4 off EMOL
- Help with inside release of #1
- Expand with #2 through the slant area if he releases to your side

- If you do not have work, (#1 outside release and #2 away or block) get immediate depth and help with verticals. Make QB put air under the ball.

Mac: Alignment 00 over the center
- Watch for exchanges to the side the running back expands to.
- Game plan ideas for 00 player
    - Read blitz when running back blocks
    - Watch for screens
    - Spy/contain quarterback

Common Routes vs. Rat

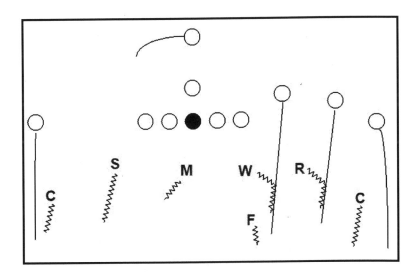

Figure 3-28. Four Verticals. The Corner plays in between #1 and #2. Free play #3 vertical. The Rover controls #2. The Will Controls #3.

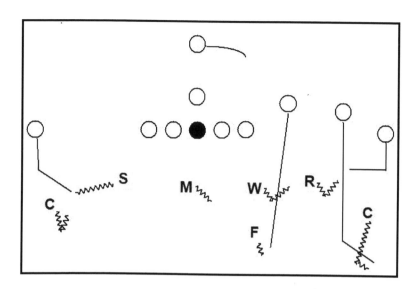

Figure 3-29. In, Corner, Vertical. The Corner calls in and takes #2 man. The Rover getting the in call comes off #2 and plays the in route. He would expand if the Corner called hitch. The Free plays #3 vertical. The Will getting the in call comes off #3 and opens to the QB and reads his shoulders and eyes.

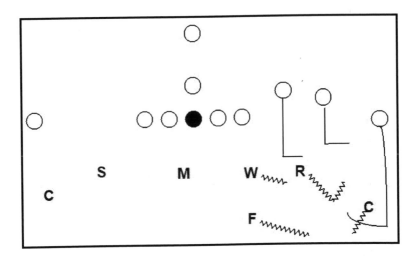

Figure 3-30. Curl, Out, Out. The Corner plays on top of #1. The Rover seeing #2 go to the flat, plays the curl and then rallies to the flat once the QB starts his throwing motion. The Will must expand when #3 expands.

4 SPLIT FIELD TRIPS ADUJSTMENTS

The third word in our call system is our adjustment to trips. Again, this system allows the coach to tailor each specific call to meet his needs. We use the tools given in the Split Field Basics chapter to play trips. There are two basic ways we play trips using split field coverage. We bring the Rover's eyes to the frontside (the trips side) effectively playing 4 over 3 on the frontside and 2 over 2 on the backside or leave the Rover' eyes backside allowing us to play 3 over 2 backside and 3 over 3 frontside. Backside calls are generally better versus the run as it allows the Rover, in certain situations, to play closer to the line of scrimmage.

Our frontside calls include: Solo, Duo, Macho and Trio
Our backside calls include: Special, Solid and Cover 3

Frontside Trips Calls

Solo

Play Read to #1 and #2 with the Corner, Free and the Sam. The Rover has #3 man to man if he releases vertical. If #3 releases outside the Rover should look for a new #3 vertical. If #3 releases inside under the LB's, the Rover should help with #1 weak. The Mac must wall any #3 low and not let him cross the formation. Remember, the Sam still has curl to swing of #3. The Will is man to man on the back and the Corner is man to man on #1 to his side. Note: Some coaches also call this Poach.

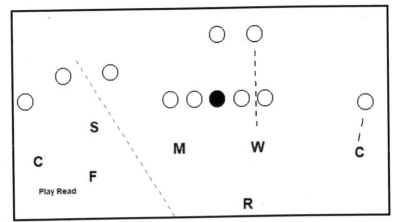

Figure 4-1. Solo.

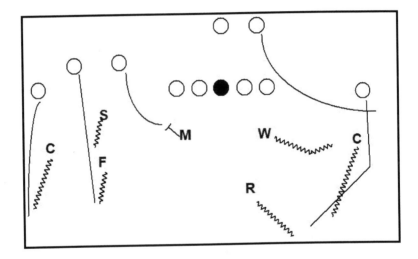

Figure 4-2. Low Crosser. The Mac must handle any low #3 crosser as it is possible for the offense to pull his help away from him with a swing of the RB.

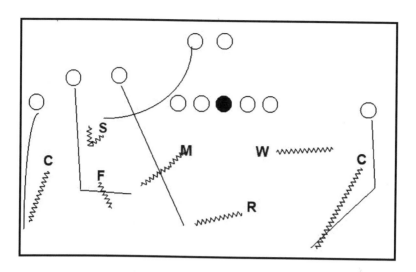

Figure 4-3. Sam must handle the new swing of #3. The Mac sees there is not a low crosser so he can expand and deepen.

Duo

Play Trap to #1 and #2 with the Corner, Free and the Sam. The Rover has #3 man to man if he releases vertical. If #3 releases outside the Rover should look for a new #3. If #3 releases inside, the Rover should help with #1 weak. The Mac must wall any #3 low and not let him cross the formation. The Will is man to man on the back and the Corner is man to man on the wide receiver.

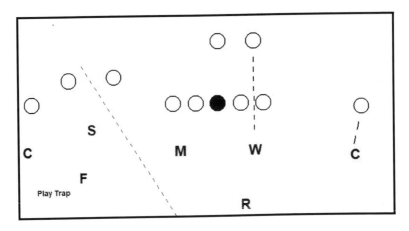

Figure 4-4. Duo. Same as Solo except the Corner, Free, and Sam play trap.

Macho

Play Blue to #1 and #2 with the Corner, Free. The Rover and the Sam banjo #3, meaning if #3 goes out, the Sam will have him man to man, if #3 releases vertical, the Rover will take him man to man. The Will is man to man on the back and the Corner is man to man on the wide receiver. We play this coverage when #3 is lined up as a TE or near the TE position. This allows the Sam to play closer to the core of the formation to better help with force and also allows the Rover to better help out on weak run.

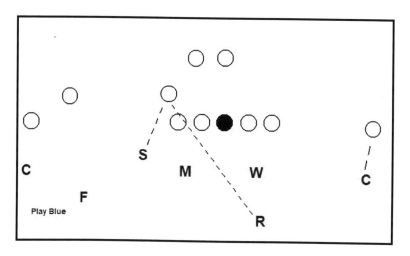

Figure 4-5. Macho.

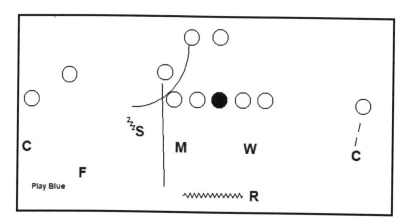

Figure 4-6. Macho #3 and #4 switch. Sam is in good position to help with force and take any immediate threat to the flat.

Backside Trips Calls

Special

Corner to trips plays man on #1. The Sam and the Free play "Read" over #2 and #3. The Mac plays curl to swing of #4. The Rover, Corner and the Will play Sky. The Rover is the force player on the weak side. If #3 were to go out, the Free makes a "jump" call. We do not make an "out" call because it was confusing to our young corners.

Note : Many coaches substitute a Nickel for the Sam in this situation. We don't do this because we have found that, at least for us in high school, the Sam is a better cover guy than our 5th best defensive back. Many coaches call this Stubbie

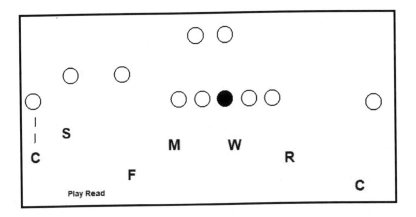

Figure 4- 7. Special. The Rover and the Mac are force players.

Solid

Corner to trips plays man on #1. The Sam and the Free play "Read" over #2 and #3. The Mac plays curl to swing of #4. The Corner and Will play man like in Solo. (Solid and Solo both begin with "So). The Rover is now a free player for you to do as you please by game plan.

Ideas we have used include: read the QB's eyes for pass, spy an athletic QB, double team #1, blitz, and "be a point man hitter".

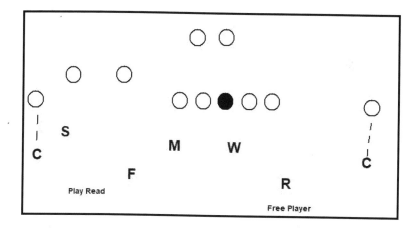

Figure 4-8. Solid. Mac and Rover are force players.

Cover 3

Cover 3 is played exactly like Rat except that the trips is to Sam instead of the Rover

Corner to trips- Align between the bottom of the #'s and the sideline no closer than 5 yards from the boundary.

- Play deep 1/3
- Be a deep as the deepest and in the middle of both #1 and #2 if both release vertical. Be alert for #2 and #3 deep crossing
- Do not chase post
- Call in or hitch to the apex player if necessary. You have the remaining player deep man to man.

Sam- Alignment: Apex #2 and #3 5 yards deep
- Wall, collision and carry #2 vertical
- Come off any vertical when *in or hitch* is called by the corner.
- If #2 outside releases, play curl to flat. Playing curl to flat means that the apex player plays the curl until the quarterback's shoulders and eyes turn to the flat route. Do not run with the wheel player.

Mac- Alignment: 50 over the OT
- Control #3
- Come off and play any *in* calls made by the corner or a safety
- If #3 outside releases play hook to curl

Will: Alignment 00 over the center
- Watch for exchanges to the side the running back expands to.
- Game plan ideas for 00 player
  - Read blitz when running back blocks
  - Watch for screens
  - Spy/contain quarterback

Rover: Alignment: 4x4 off EMOL
- Help with inside release of #1
- Expand with #2 through the slant area if he releases to your side
- If you do not have work, (#1 outside release and #2 away or block) get immediate depth and help with verticals. Make quarterback put air under the ball.

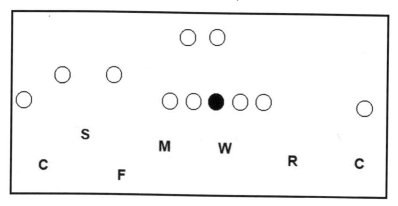

Figure 4-9. Cover 3. Mac and Rover are force players.

5 SPLIT FIELD OTHER FORMATIONS

Empty Ideas

Empty formations are handled within our system using concepts provided in the Split Basics chapter and the Trips Adjustments chapter. When an "Empty, Empty" check is made. The concept is: we will always play 4 over 3 to three receivers and 3 over 2 versus two receivers unless a blitz is called. The Free has a choice to call Special, 3, or Read. If the Free has two receivers, he will call Read. If he has 3 receivers, he will call Special or 3, depending on game plan or personnel.

The Rover has a choice to call Blue or 3 Pull. If the Rover has 2 receivers, he calls "Blue". If he has 3 receivers, he calls "3 Pull. The pull is to alert the next linebacker to apex #2 and #3. The linebacker could be a Will or a Buck depending if we are in a 3 or 4 down look. Note: Unless blitzing, the Rover will not be a box player.

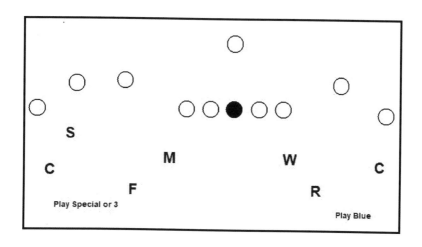

Figure 5-1. 3x2 The Free calls Read or Special. The Rover calls Blue.

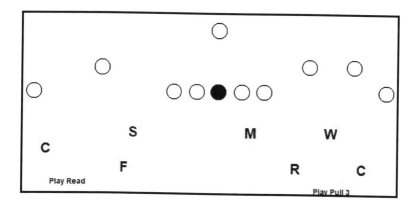

Figure 5-2. 2x3 The Free calls Read. The Rover calls 3 Pull, pulling the Will out of the core.

Quads (4 receivers to a side) can be played by having the Corner play man on #1. The Sam, Free and Mac play Special over #2 and #3. The Mac is the new curl to swing of #4 player. The Will and the Rover play Solo on #4. The backside Corner is man on #1 weak. If you are concerned

41

about having your backside Corner cover #1, play a 3 down look and "walk" the Buck over #1 and have him press. We call that "Butter" and is called from the sideline. If you do not like man coverage you could also rush 3 and play cover 3.

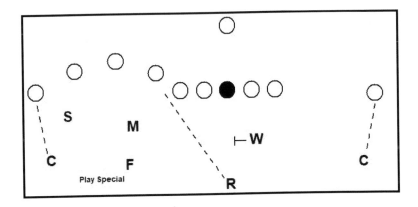

Figure 5-3. Quads with a Solo call. The Corners are Man. The Sam and the Free play Special. The Mac must wall any low crossing routes. The Rover is man on any #4 vertical.

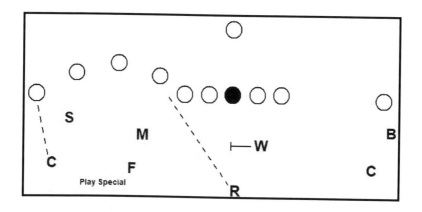

Figure 5-4. Quads with a Butter call. (3 down look)

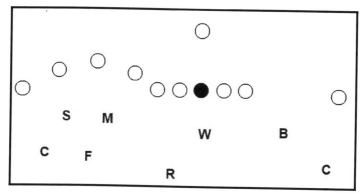

Figure 5-5. Quads with Cover 3 (3 down look)

Bunch Formation Ideas

Bunch formations can be played multiple ways: As with other trips formations, we need to make a decision whether we need to involve the Rover in the coverage to the trips or help with coverage and run support away from trips. We do play Cover 3, Solo, and Duo to Bunch but have also added Box and 3 Roll. Box allows us to keep the Rover backside while 3 Roll brings (rolls) the Rover frontside.

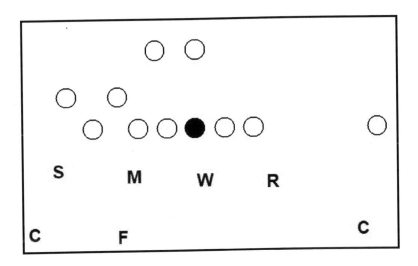

Figure 5-6. Box. Sam has first out low, Mac has first in low the Corner has first deep outside and the Free has first deep inside. This creates our box.

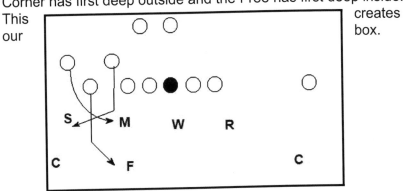

Figure 5-6A. Box

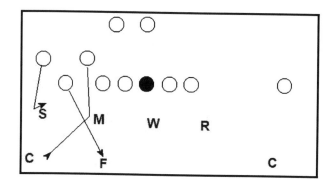

Figure 5-6B. Box

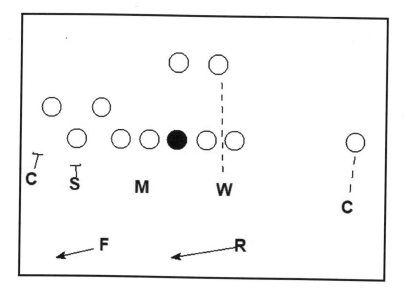

Figure 5-7. 3 Roll. The frontside Corner is the flat player, The Sam jams and plays the curl, the Mac controls #3 as described in the Split Basics chapter. The Free is the outside ⅓ player, the Rover is middle ⅓ player. The Will and the backside corner play

just like Solo. The coverage is great versus teams that like to use compressed formations to run to the field.

Cloud Check Ideas

Against certain teams, we will go into the game with a Cloud check. We like this on run downs versus Wing-T teams in conjunction with our Under Front Defense which is described in my previous book. The Cloud check is played very similar to our Trap call except now the Corner aligns 2 yards deep and 1-2 two yards outside the receiver. The Corner cannot allow an outside release. If the receiver manages to release outside the Corner now must take him man.

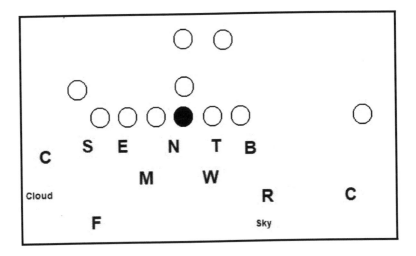

Figure 5-8. The free makes a Cloud call versus a Wing-T formation. Corner is now the force player.

We will also make a Special Cloud call as a trips tag. This means that the Rover calls Special Cloud when the offense presents a trips formation. This is especially helpful against teams that put their best player away from the trips hoping to get man to man coverage.

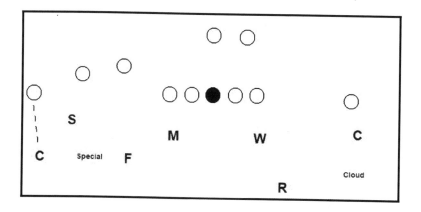

Figure 5-9. Special cloud. The Rover makes a Special Cloud call.

Handling a Star Ideas

We use the terms Mustard, Jam, and Butter to designate players to align and press a receiver. When Jam is called, the Sam will press #2 to his side. When Butter is called, the Buck will press #1 to his side. When Mustard is called, the Mac will press #3. Examples of a huddle call would include: Field Jam Read Choice Solo, Under Mustard Will Plug Read Choice Special. The Mac would not "Mustard" #3 unless it were trips. We only call Butter when we are in our 3-4 (Okie) alignment.

We call Star when we want to have our Sam or our Buck "Press" the star receiver to his side of the ball.

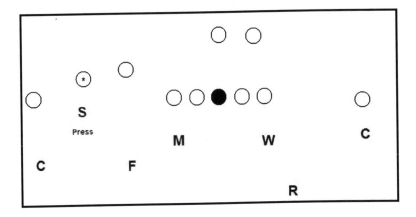

Figure 5-10. Star with a Jam Call

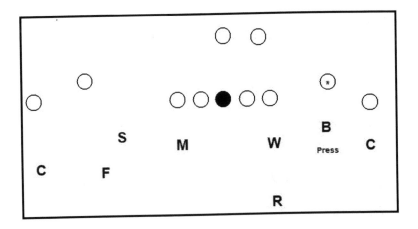

Figure 5-11 Star with a Butter Call

Another way we game plan against a "Star" is to adjust our coverage to him. We call this "Hunt". The call would be "Field Hunt".

If the Star is aligned at #1 we would check Trap (or Duo if its trips). We could also add the term "Press" to the call.

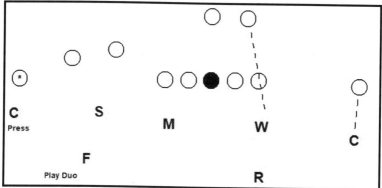

Figure 5-12. Check Trap or Duo if aligned at #1 strong.

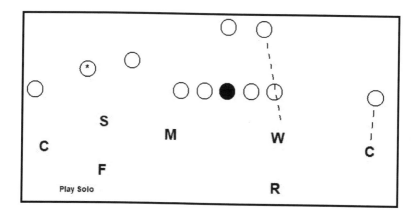

Figure 5-13. Check Solo if the Star is frontside #2. Align the Sam close to the Star. We could also align the Sam outside of #2 and play it similar to our Robber concept discussed in the Chapter 3.

If the "Star" is aligned at #3 to the trips, we would play Macho .

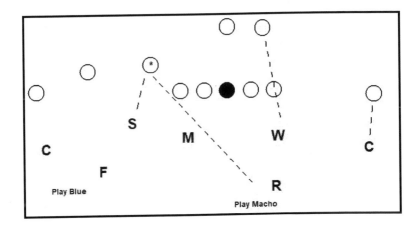

Figure 5-14. Check Macho if the star is aligned at #3

If the "Star" is aligned at #1 away from trips we would check Special Cloud. We could also make a "Butter" call if the Star were aligned at #1 away from the trips.

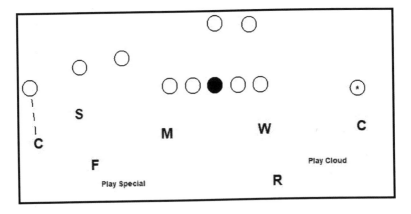

Figure 5-15. Check Special Cloud if the Star is aligned at #1 away from trips.

6 SPLIT FIELD BLITZ COVERAGES

Split field coverages are also used when we blitz. A sample call would be Field House Purple Choice Rock. Using our structure from the Split Field Basics chapter. Field would be the front, House would be the blitz, Purple would be the read side call, Choice would be the away side call and Rock would be the trips check.

Calls include: Purple, Rock, Paper and Trio

Purple

Purple is a deeper shade of blue. The read side now plays Blue coverage. The away side, again, is given a choice of Blue, Sky or Rat. Purple also indicates that the outermost rusher will "peel" and cover any flaring receiver from the backfield. Purple equals "peel". Receivers releasing through the line of scrimmage must be tackled by the inside linebackers.

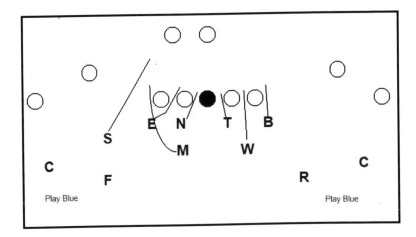

Figure 6-1. Blue is played to both sides.

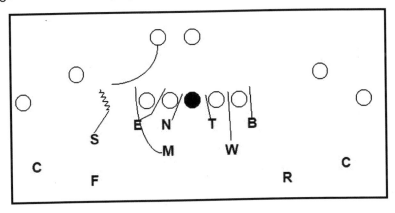

Figure 6-2. The most outside rusher, in this case the Sam, must "peel" off when a receiver exits the backfield.

Rock

Rock is played exactly like Cover 3 as described in the Split Field Trips chapter. The Free now "rocks" down walls, collisions and carries #2 vertical. The Rover "rocks" over and becomes the middle ⅓ player.

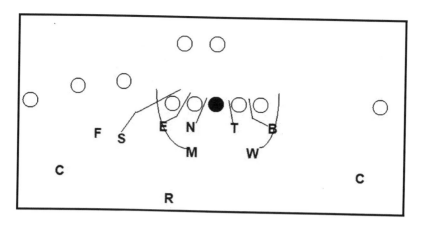

Figure 6-3. The Free rocks down and the Rover rocks over

Paper

Paper is played exactly Special on the trips side and Solo on the away side except now the Free is the Sam and the Rover becomes the Free. Note: We do not play this coverage but some high school teams do.

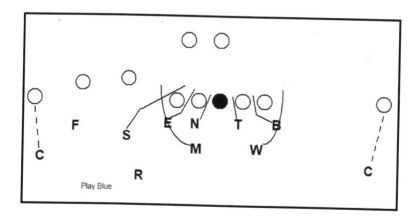

Figure 6-4. The Free and Rover play Blue.

Trio

Trio is a coverage used when blitzing the Sam. Play Blue to #1 and #2 with the Corner, Free safety. The Rover has #3 man to man. The Sam is on a blitz . We play this coverage when #3 is lined up as a TE or near the TE position.

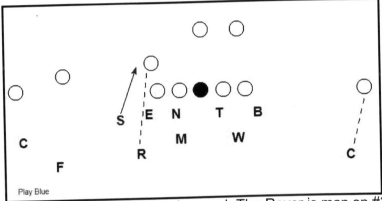

Play Blue

Figure 6-5. Free and Corner play read, The Rover is man on #3.

7 SPLIT FIELD COVERAGES VS. RPO'S

We generally see 4 different types of options. Zone Read, Power Read, Speed Option and Veer Option. We feel that if a HS offense is willing commit 7 to run option then we will commit 7 to defend against the option. Our "box" players are always assigned to stop the run first and then react to the pass. We do not assign defenders to the running back or the quarterback. Instead, we have defenders assigned to a "high player" and a "low player". Although we might have an idea of who the high and low player will be before the snap of the ball, teams can switch up their high and low players from the same look in the backfield. Zone read and speed option can look exactly the same BEFORE the play starts. We must be precise with our assignments and alignments.

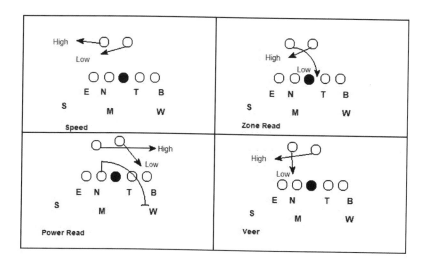

Figure 7-1. High and Low Player designations.

The huddle call is Field Read Choice Special. The Free will play Read, The Rover is given a choice of Blue or Sky and we will play Special to any trips. Unless called in the huddle, the Sam is the

"High" player to his side, the End and Mac are low players. Note: the End and Buck are "spill" or block down, step down" players. (More info about defensive line play can be found at www.CoachJerryGordon.com). To the away side, the Will is the "High" player when Blue is called by the Rover.

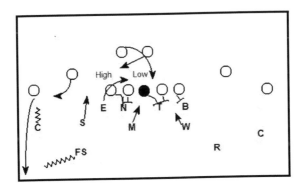

Figure 7-2. Zone Read to the Sam. Sam is high player. Mac and End are low players. The Free would make an "out" call.

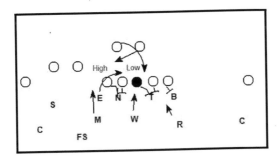

Figure 7-3. Zone Read to trips. The Mac aligns in a 50 and is now the high player. The End and the Will are low players. The Free makes a Special check. The Rover calls Sky and is the force (high) player to his side.

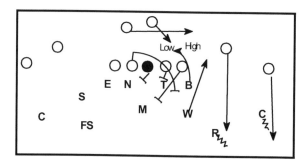

Figure 7-4. Power Read to the Will. The Rover calls Blue because he has 2 receivers to his side. The Buck is the low player (QB). The Will is the high player (RB).

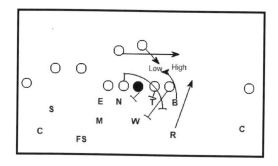

Figure 7-5. Power Read away from trips. The Trips check is Special. The Buck is the low player (QB) and the Rover, in a Sky check is the high player (QB).

Another way we play run/pass options is with a "Robber" call to the field. This puts the Sam in a position to play a bubble pass or a "now" screen to his side. The Free safety becomes the high player to his side.

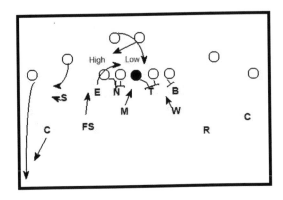

Figure 7-6. Robber Choice Special. The Free Safety checks Robber and is the high player. The Rover is playing Blue to his side.

We could also play with a Cover 3 call as our trips check. The idea being we want to keep the Rover backside to be the force player vs trips.

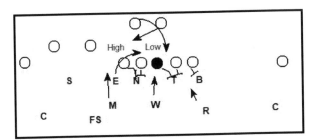

Figure 7-7. Cover 3 check to trips.

8 SPLIT FIELD COVERAGE RESOURCES

Everything I have shown in this book has been learned from someone else. I have been able to take these ideas and package them to suit my own needs. The following are resources that have been helpful:

CoachJerryGordon.com

Complete Linebacking - Lou Tepper

Football's Eagle and Stack Defenses - Ron Vanderlinden

Quarters Coverage Made Simple - Shap Boyd

CoachHuey.com

Blitzology.com

MatchQuarters.com

XandOsLab.com

CoachHoover.blogspot.com

Footballislifeblog.blogspot.com

Smartfootball.com

USAFootball.com

JamesLightFootball.com

BrophyFootball.blogspot.com

ABOUT THE AUTHOR

Jerry Gordon is currently the defensive coordinator at Nauset Regional High School located in Eastham, MA. Gordon started his football career as a walk-on at University of Massachusetts in 1979. He went on to become a three year starter on the offensive line, earning a full scholarship and becoming one of the only few players in University of Massachusetts history to become a two-time captain. University of Massachusetts won or shared 3 Yankee Conference football championships in that period.

Gordon has coached with the Boston Breakers (USFL), Northeastern University, University of Massachusetts, Yale University, Sandwich (MA) High School, Potomac Falls (VA) High School, Woodgrove (VA) High School and Broad Run (VA) High School.

Gordon has had two articles published in Gridiron Magazine and an article published in Success Magazine. Gordon has also written numerous Internet articles, has appeared on Portland Radio Station 95.5 "The Game" and on USA Football's Coach and Coordinator Podcast with Keith Grabowski.

Gordon and his wife Carol, currently reside in Chatham, MA. Gordon is stepfather to two children, Erik and Jennifer, and has four granddaughters: Ella, Beatrice, Macie, and Kendall.

Gordon can be reached at jgordon0508@yahoo.com.

@JerryGordonFB

Made in the USA
Middletown, DE
29 March 2019